Simple ABC Book

By: Ilonah Angel

Letters

Aa Bb Cc Dd Ee

Ff Gg Hh Ii Jj Kk

Ll Mm Nn Oo Pp

Qq Rr Ss Tt Uu

Vv Ww Xx Yy Zz

/ei/

A is for ant.

A is for anchor.

A is for apple.

/bee/

B is for bird.

B is for ball.

Bb

B is for balloons

B is for bee.

/cee/

C is for cookies.

C is for cake.

C is for cat.

/dee/

D is for dinosaurs.

Dd

D is for duck.

D is for dog.

/e/

E is for eggs.

E is for earth.

Ee

E is for elephant.

/ef/

F is for fish.

Ff

F is for fox.

F is for frog.

/gee/

G is for gift.

Gg

G is for giraffes.

G is for grapes.

/aitch/

H is for heart.
H is for hat.
Hh
H is for house.

/i/

I is for ink.
ink
I is for iguana.
Ii
I is for ice cream.

/jay/

J is for juice.

J is for jam.

Jj

J is for jellyfish.

/kay/

K is for kiwi.

K is for key.

K is for kangaroos.

/ el /

L is for ladybug.

Ll

L is for leaf.

/em/

M is for moon.

Mm

M is for mushroom.

/en/

N is for nurse.

Nn

N is for noodles.

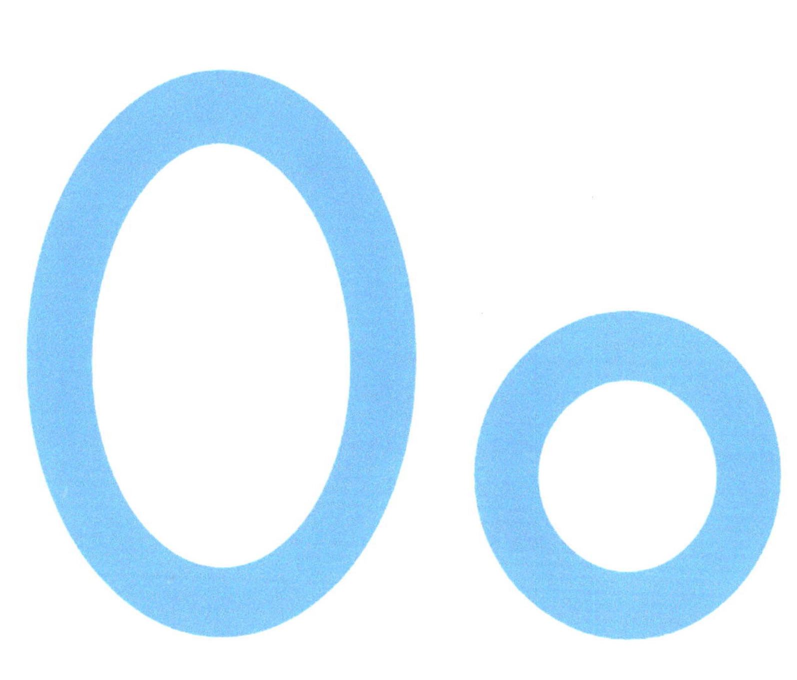

/ou/

O is for octopus.

Oo

O is for orange.

/pi/

P is for panda.
Pp
P is for pig.

/kiu/

Q is for question.

Q is for quail.

Rr

/ar/

R is for rain.

R is for rose.

R is for rainbow.

/es/

S is for sun.

Ss

S is for strawberry.

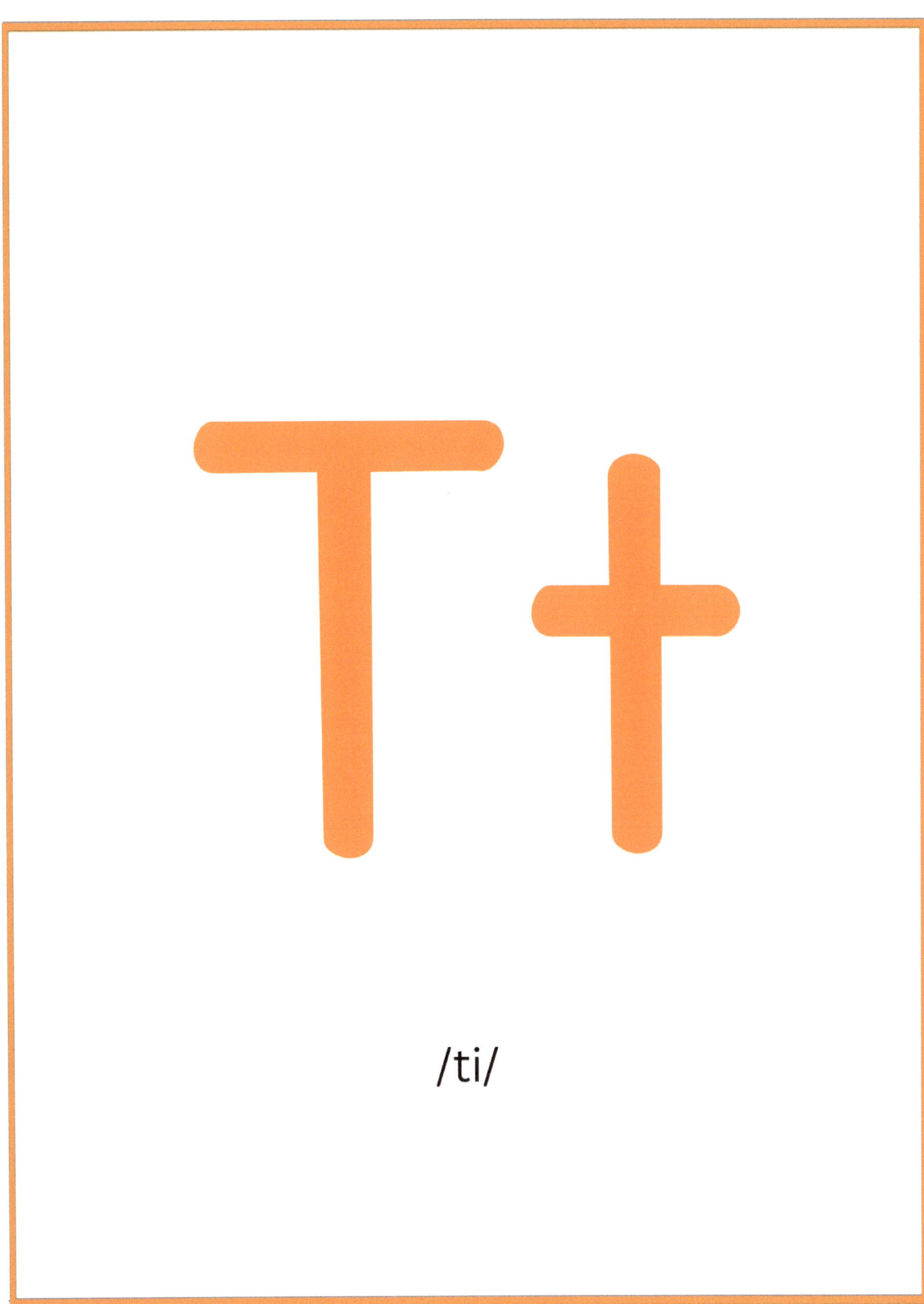
Tt
/ti/

T is for tomatoes.

Tt

T is for turtle.

/yu/

U is for umbrella.

Uu

U is for unicorn.

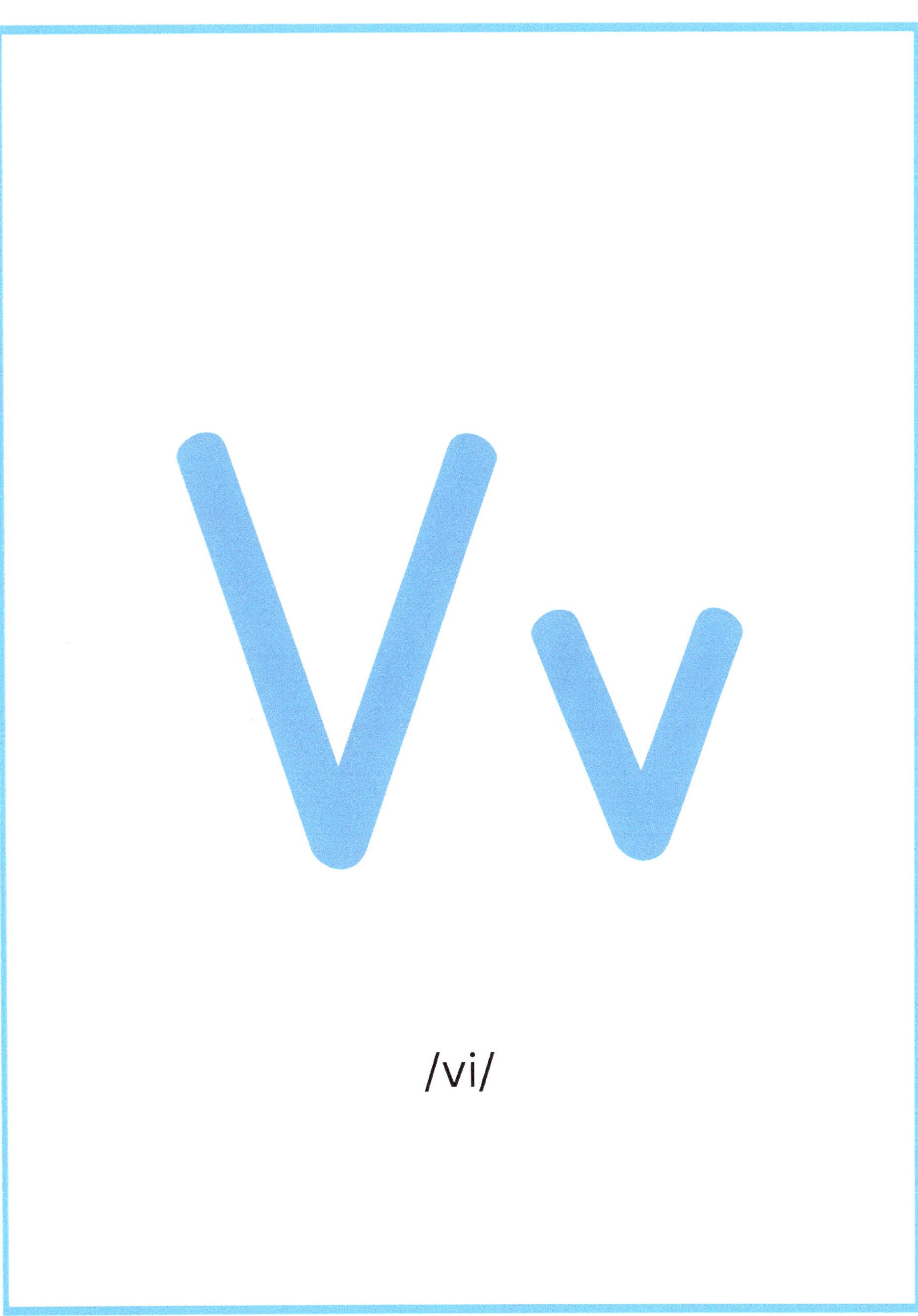
Vv
/vi/

V is for violin.
Vv
V is for van.
V is for vase.

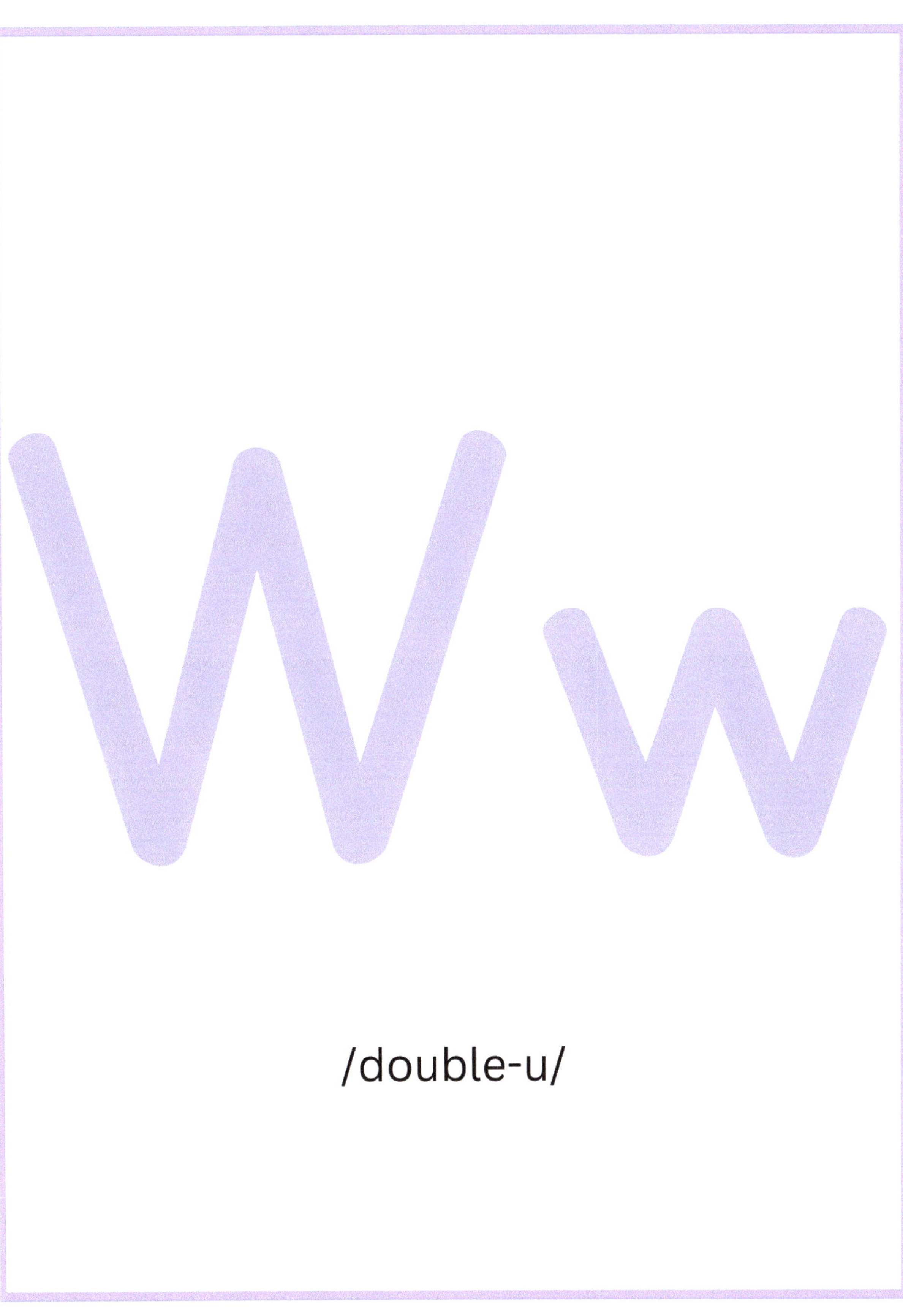

/double-u/

W is for watermelon.

Ww

W is for worm.

W is for whale.

/ecs/

X is for x-ray.

/wy/

Y is for yogurt.

Yy

Y is for yo-yo.

Zz

/zee/

Z is for zebra.

Zz

Z is for zipper.

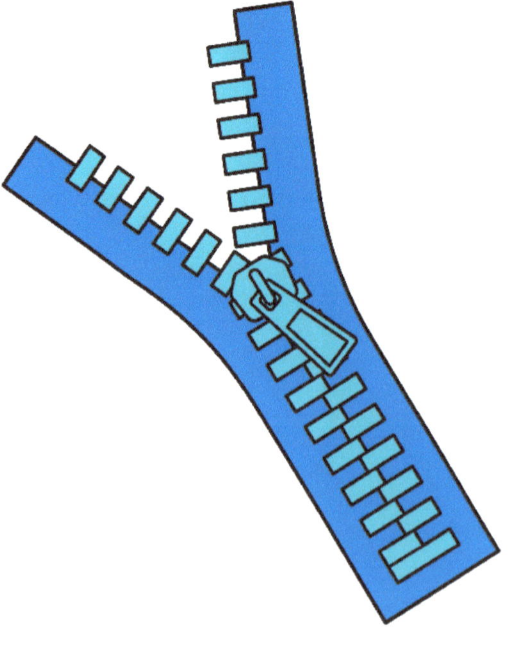

www.ingramcontent.com/pod-product-compliance
Lightning Source LLC
LaVergne TN
LVHW071125160826
845679LV00005B/1178

* 9 7 9 8 3 5 5 4 9 2 1 4 4 *